The BIG BOOK of
horn songs

D1482263

Note: The keys in this book do not match the other wind instruments.

AVAILABLE FOR:

Flute, Clarinet, Alto Sax, Tenor Sax, Trumpet,
Horn, Trombone, Violin, Viola, and Cello

ISBN-13: 978-1-4234-2668-4
ISBN-10: 1-4234-2668-1

HAL•LEONARD®
CORPORATION
7777 W. BLUEMOUND RD. P.O. BOX 13819 MILWAUKEE, WI 53213

Visit Hal Leonard Online at
www.halleonard.com

ALL MY LOVING
from A HARD DAY'S NIGHT

Horn

Words and Music by JOHN LENNON
and PAUL McCARTNEY

ALL THE SMALL THINGS

Horn

Words and Music by TOM DE LONGE
and MARK HOPPUS

ALLEY CAT

HORN

By FRANK BJORN

ANOTHER ONE BITES THE DUST

Horn

Words and Music by
JOHN DEACON

8

AMERICA
from the Motion Picture THE JAZZ SINGER

Horn

Words and Music by
NEIL DIAMOND

ANY DREAM WILL DO

from JOSEPH AND THE AMAZING TECHNICOLOR® DREAMCOAT

Horn

Music by ANDREW LLOYD WEBBER
Lyrics by TIM RICE

BE TRUE TO YOUR SCHOOL

Horn

Words and Music by BRIAN WILSON
and MIKE LOVE

BAD DAY

Horn

Words and Music by
DANIEL POWTER

D.S. al Coda

CODA

BARELY BREATHING

HORN

Words and Music by
DUNCAN SHEIK

(It's A)
BEAUTIFUL MORNING

HORN

Words and Music by FELIX CAVALIERE
and EDWARD BRIGATI, JR.

BEAUTY AND THE BEAST

from Walt Disney's BEAUTY AND THE BEAST

Lyrics by HOWARD ASHMAN
Music by ALAN MENKEN

HORN

BEYOND THE SEA

HORN

Words and Music by CHARLES TRENET,
ALBERT LASRY and JACK LAWRENCE

BLACKBIRD

Horn

Words and Music by JOHN LENNON
and PAUL McCARTNEY

Slowly and smoothly

BLUE SUEDE SHOES

HORN

Words and Music by
CARL LEE PERKINS

BOOGIE WOOGIE BUGLE BOY

from BUCK PRIVATES

Horn

Words and Music by DON RAYE
and HUGHIE PRINCE

THE BRADY BUNCH
Theme from the Paramount Television Series THE BRADY BUNCH

HORN

Words and Music by SHERWOOD SCHWARTZ
and FRANK DEVOL

BUTTERFLY KISSES

Horn

Words and Music by BOB CARLISLE
and RANDY THOMAS

BREAKING FREE

from the Disney Channel Original Movie HIGH SCHOOL MUSICAL

HORN

Words and Music by
JAMIE HOUSTON

Moderately

CABARET
from the Musical CABARET

HORN

Words by FRED EBB
Music by JOHN KANDER

Lively

CALIFORNIA DREAMIN'

Horn

Words and Music by JOHN PHILLIPS
and MICHELLE PHILLIPS

Medium Rock beat

CANDLE IN THE WIND

Horn

Words and Music by ELTON JOHN
and BERNIE TAUPIN

Slow 2

CHIM CHIM CHER-EE
from Walt Disney's MARY POPPINS

Horn

Words and Music by RICHARD M. SHERMAN
and ROBERT B. SHERMAN

Lightly, with gusto

small notes optional

CLOCKS

Horn

Words and Music by GUY BERRYMAN, JON BUCKLAND,
WILL CHAMPION and CHRIS MARTIN

(They Long to Be)
CLOSE TO YOU

Horn

Lyric by HAL DAVID
Music by BURT BACHARACH

Slowly, with a steady beat

COLORS OF THE WIND

from Walt Disney's POCAHONTAS

Horn

Music by ALAN MENKEN
Lyrics by STEPHEN SCHWARTZ

COME FLY WITH ME

HORN

Words by SAMMY CAHN
Music by JAMES VAN HEUSEN

Moderate Swing

COPACABANA
(At the Copa)
from Barry Manilow's COPACABANA

HORN

Music by BARRY MANILOW
Lyric by BRUCE SUSSMAN and JACK FELDMAN

DO-RE-MI
from THE SOUND OF MUSIC

Horn

Lyrics by OSCAR HAMMERSTEIN II
Music by RICHARD RODGERS

DO WAH DIDDY DIDDY

Horn

Words and Music by JEFF BARRY
and ELLIE GREENWICH

(Sittin' On)
THE DOCK OF THE BAY

HORN

Words and Music by STEVE CROPPER
and OTIS REDDING

DON'T BE CRUEL
(To a Heart That's True)

Horn

Words and Music by OTIS BLACKWELL
and ELVIS PRESLEY

DON'T LET THE SUN GO DOWN ON ME

Horn

Words and Music by ELTON JOHN
and BERNIE TAUPIN

Slow Rock

DON'T SPEAK

HORN

Words and Music by ERIC STEFANI
and GWEN STEFANI

DRIFT AWAY

HORN

Words and Music by
MENTOR WILLIAMS

Moderately fast

To Coda

D.C. al Coda

CODA

DUKE OF EARL

Horn

Words and Music by EARL EDWARDS,
EUGENE DIXON and BERNICE WILLIAMS

THEME FROM E.T. (THE EXTRA-TERRESTRIAL)

from the Universal Picture E.T. (THE EXTRA-TERRESTRIAL)

Horn

Music by
JOHN WILLIAMS

EDELWEISS
from THE SOUND OF MUSIC

Horn

Lyrics by OSCAR HAMMERSTEIN II
Music by RICHARD RODGERS

EVERY BREATH YOU TAKE

HORN

Music and Lyrics by
STING

Medium Rock

EVERYTHING IS BEAUTIFUL

HORN

Words and Music by
RAY STEVENS

Moderately fast

FALLIN'

HORN

Words and Music by
ALICIA KEYS

FIELDS OF GOLD

HORN

Music and Lyrics by
STING

FLY LIKE AN EAGLE

Horn

Words and Music by
STEVE MILLER

Moderately, in 2

FOR ONCE IN MY LIFE

HORN

Words by RONALD MILLER
Music by ORLANDO MURDEN

Slowly, with feeling

FOREVER YOUNG

Horn

Words and Music by ROD STEWART,
JIM CREGAN, KEVIN SAVIGAR and BOB DYLAN

FUN, FUN, FUN

HORN

Words and Music by BRIAN WILSON
and MIKE LOVE

Bright Rock

THE GIRL FROM IPANEMA
(Garôta de Ipanema)

Horn

Music by ANTONIO CARLOS JOBIM
English Words by NORMAN GIMBEL
Original Words by VINICIUS DE MORAES

GOD BLESS THE U.S.A

Horn

Words and Music by
LEE GREENWOOD

GONNA BUILD A MOUNTAIN

from the Musical Production STOP THE WORLD – I WANT TO GET OFF

Horn

Words and Music by LESLIE BRICUSSE
and ANTHONY NEWLEY

Moderately bright

GOODBYE YELLOW BRICK ROAD

Horn

Words and Music by ELTON JOHN
and BERNIE TAUPIN

Moderately slow, in 2

GREEN GREEN GRASS OF HOME

HORN

Words and Music by
CURLY PUTMAN

HAPPY DAYS
Theme from the Paramount Television Series HAPPY DAYS

HORN

Words by NORMAN GIMBEL
Music by CHARLES FOX

HAVE I TOLD YOU LATELY

Horn

Words and Music by
VAN MORRISON

HEART AND SOUL
from the Paramount Short Subject A SONG IS BORN

Horn

Words by FRANK LOESSER
Music by HOAGY CARMICHAEL

Moderately, lightly rhythmical

HOGAN'S HEROES MARCH
from the Television Series HOGAN'S HEROES

Horn

By JERRY FIELDING

HERE WITHOUT YOU

Horn

Words and Music by MATT ROBERTS,
BRAD ARNOLD, CHRISTOPHER HENDERSON
and ROBERT HARRELL

I DREAMED A DREAM
from LES MISÉRABLES

Horn

Music by CLAUDE-MICHEL SCHÖNBERG
Lyrics by ALAIN BOUBLIL, JEAN-MARC NATEL
and HERBERT KRETZMER

I HEARD IT THROUGH THE GRAPEVINE

Horn

Words and Music by NORMAN J. WHITFIELD
and BARRETT STRONG

I SAY A LITTLE PRAYER

HORN

Lyric by HAL DAVID
Music by BURT BACHARACH

I WHISTLE A HAPPY TUNE

from THE KING AND I

Horn

Lyrics by OSCAR HAMMERSTEIN II
Music by RICHARD RODGERS

Brightly

I WILL REMEMBER YOU
Theme from THE BROTHERS McMULLEN

Horn

Words and Music by SARAH McLACHLAN,
SEAMUS EGAN and DAVE MERENDA

I WRITE THE SONGS

Horn

Words and Music by
BRUCE JOHNSTON

Slow Ballad

I'M POPEYE THE SAILOR MAN

Theme from the Paramount Cartoon POPEYE THE SAILOR

Horn

Words and Music by
SAMMY LERNER

IF I EVER LOSE MY FAITH IN YOU

Horn

Music and Lyrics by
STING

IMAGINE

HORN

Words and Music by
JOHN LENNON

Medium slow

IT'S MY LIFE

Horn

Words and Music by JON BON JOVI,
RICHARD SAMBORA and MARTIN SANDBERG

Moderately

IT'S STILL ROCK AND ROLL TO ME

HORN

Words and Music by
BILLY JOEL

JAILHOUSE ROCK

Horn

Words and Music by JERRY LEIBER
and MIKE STOLLER

JOY TO THE WORLD

HORN

Words and Music by
HOYT AXTON

Moderate Gospel Rock

JUMP, JIVE AN' WAIL

Horn

Words and Music by
LOUIS PRIMA

KANSAS CITY

Horn

Words and Music by JERRY LEIBER
and MIKE STOLLER

KOKOMO
from the Motion Picture COCKTAIL

Horn

Words and Music by MIKE LOVE, TERRY MELCHER,
JOHN PHILLIPS and SCOTT McKENZIE

Moderately bright

To Coda

D.S. al Coda

CODA

LET 'EM IN

HORN

Words and Music by
PAUL and LINDA McCARTNEY

LET'S STAY TOGETHER

Horn

Words and Music by AL GREEN,
WILLIE MITCHELL and AL JACKSON, JR.

Moderate Rock

D.C. al Coda

CODA

LIKE A ROCK

HORN

Words and Music by
BOB SEGER

LIVIN' LA VIDA LOCA

HORN

Words and Music by ROBI ROSA
and DESMOND CHILD

Fast, with a steady beat

LOVE AND MARRIAGE

Words by SAMMY CAHN
Music by JAMES VAN HEUSEN

Horn

LOVE STORY
Theme from the Paramount Picture LOVE STORY

HORN

Music by FRANCIS LAI

MAGGIE MAY

Horn

Words and Music by ROD STEWART
and MARTIN QUITTENTON

Moderately bright

MAKING OUR DREAMS COME TRUE
Theme from the Paramount Television Series LAVERNE AND SHIRLEY

Words by NORMAN GIMBEL
Music by CHARLES FOX

HORN

MAYBE I'M AMAZED

Words and Music by
PAUL McCARTNEY

Horn

Moderately

small notes optional

MICHELLE

HORN

Words and Music by JOHN LENNON
and PAUL McCARTNEY

MICKEY MOUSE MARCH

from Walt Disney's THE MICKEY MOUSE CLUB

Horn

Words and Music by
JIMMIE DODD

MISSION: IMPOSSIBLE THEME

From the Paramount Television Series MISSION: IMPOSSIBLE

HORN

By LALO SCHIFRIN

MISTER SANDMAN

Horn

Lyric and Music by
PAT BALLARD

MOON RIVER

from the Paramount Picture BREAKFAST AT TIFFANY'S

HORN

Words by JOHNNY MERCER
Music by HENRY MANCINI

MY HEART WILL GO ON
(Love Theme from 'Titanic')
from the Paramount and Twentieth Century Fox Motion Picture TITANIC

HORN

Music by JAMES HORNER
Lyric by WILL JENNINGS

MY WAY

Horn

English Words by PAUL ANKA
Original French Words by GILLES THIBAULT
Music by JACQUES REVAUX and CLAUDE FRANCOIS

NA NA HEY HEY KISS HIM GOODBYE

Horn

Words and Music by ARTHUR FRASHUER DALE,
PAUL ROGER LEKA and GARY CARLA

ON BROADWAY

HORN

Words and Music by BARRY MANN,
CYNTHIA WEIL, MIKE STOLLER and JERRY LEIBER

PEPPERMINT TWIST

Horn

Words and Music by JOSEPH DiNICOLA
and HENRY GLOVER

POCKETFUL OF MIRACLES

HORN

Words by SAMMY CAHN
Music by JAMES VAN HEUSEN

Moderately, with a lilt

PUFF THE MAGIC DRAGON

Horn

Words and Music by LENNY LIPTON
and PETER YARROW

Moderately

PUT YOUR HAND IN THE HAND

HORN

Words and Music by
GENE MacLELLAN

QUIET NIGHTS OF QUIET STARS
(Corcovado)

Horn

English Words by GENE LEES
Original Words and Music by ANTONIO CARLOS JOBIM

Moderately slow

ROCK AROUND THE CLOCK

Horn

Words and Music by MAX C. FREEDMAN
and JIMMY DeKNIGHT

ROCK WITH YOU

Horn

Words and Music by
ROD TEMPERTON

SATIN DOLL

Horn

By DUKE ELLINGTON

Save the Best for Last

Horn

Words and Music by PHIL GALDSTON,
JON LIND and WENDY WALDMAN

THEME FROM "SCHINDLER'S LIST"

from the Universal Motion Picture SCHINDLER'S LIST

Horn

Music by JOHN WILLIAMS

SHE WILL BE LOVED

Horn

Words and Music by ADAM LEVINE
and JAMES VALENTINE

SING
from SESAME STREET

HORN

Words and Music by
JOE RAPOSO

SO LONG, FAREWELL

from THE SOUND OF MUSIC

Horn

Lyrics by OSCAR HAMMERSTEIN II
Music by RICHARD RODGERS

SOMEWHERE OUT THERE
from AN AMERICAN TAIL

Horn

Music by BARRY MANN and JAMES HORNER
Lyric by CYNTHIA WEIL

SPANISH FLEA

Horn

Words and Music by
JULIUS WECHTER

STACY'S MOM

HORN

Words and Music by CHRIS COLLINGWOOD
and ADAM SCHLESINGER

Medium Rock

SUNRISE, SUNSET
from the Musical FIDDLER ON THE ROOF

Horn

Words by SHELDON HARNICK
Music by JERRY BOCK

Moderately slow Waltz tempo

TAKE MY BREATH AWAY
(Love Theme)
from the Paramount Picture TOP GUN

Horn

Words and Music by GIORGIO MORODER
and TOM WHITLOCK

THAT'S AMORÉ
(That's Love)
from the Paramount Picture THE CADDY

HORN

Words by JACK BROOKS
Music by HARRY WARREN

THIS LAND IS YOUR LAND

Horn

Words and Music by
WOODY GUTHRIE

THOSE WERE THE DAYS

Horn

Words and Music by
GENE RASKIN

TIME AFTER TIME

Horn

Words and Music by CYNDI LAUPER
and ROB HYMAN

A THOUSAND MILES

HORN

Words and Music by
VANESSA CARLTON

TOMORROW
from the Musical Production ANNIE

Horn

Lyric by MARTIN CHARNIN
Music by CHARLES STROUSE

TOP OF THE WORLD

Horn

Words and Music by JOHN BETTIS
and RICHARD CARPENTER

TWIST AND SHOUT

Horn

Words and Music by BERT RUSSELL
and PHIL MEDLEY

UNCHAINED MELODY

Horn

Lyric by HY ZARET
Music by ALEX NORTH

UNDER THE BOARDWALK

Horn

Words and Music by ARTIE RESNICK
and KENNY YOUNG

UNITED WE STAND

Horn

Words and Music by ANTHONY TOBY HILLER
and JOHN GOODISON

132

THE WAY YOU MOVE

HORN

Words and Music by ANTWAN PATTON,
PATRICK BROWN and CARLTON MAHONE

WE ARE THE WORLD

Horn

Words and Music by LIONEL RICHIE
and MICHAEL JACKSON

WE BELONG TOGETHER

Horn

Words and Music by MARIAH CAREY,
JERMAINE DUPRI, MANUEL SEAL, JOHNTA AUSTIN,
DARNELL BRISTOL, KENNETH EDMONDS, SIDNEY JOHNSON,
PATRICK MOTEN, BOBBY WOMACK and SANDRA SULLY

Slow Soul

WHAT THE WORLD NEEDS NOW IS LOVE

Horn

Lyric by HAL DAVID
Music by BURT BACHARACH

WITH A LITTLE HELP FROM MY FRIENDS

Horn

Words and Music by JOHN LENNON
and PAUL McCARTNEY

WONDERFUL TONIGHT

HORN

Words and Music by
ERIC CLAPTON

WOOLY BULLY

Horn

Words and Music by
DOMINGO SAMUDIO

Moderately

small notes optional

YELLOW SUBMARINE

Horn

Words and Music by JOHN LENNON
and PAUL McCARTNEY

YOU ARE THE SUNSHINE OF MY LIFE

HORN

Words and Music by
STEVIE WONDER

Moderately

YOU RAISE ME UP

HORN

Words and Music by BRENDAN GRAHAM
and ROLF LOVLAND

Moderately slow

small notes optional

YOU'VE GOT A FRIEND

HORN

Words and Music by
CAROLE KING

ZIP-A-DEE-DOO-DAH

from Walt Disney's SONG OF THE SOUTH
from Disneyland and Walt Disney World's SPLASH MOUNTAIN

Horn

Words by RAY GILBERT
Music by ALLIE WRUBEL